My Australian Rules Football Journal

NAME _____

SEASON YEAR _____

TEAM NAME

_____

MY FOOTY JOURNAL

©The Life Graduate Publishing Group - 2021

No part of this book may be scanned, reproduced or distributed in any printed or electronic form without the prior permission of the author or publisher.

THE LIFE GRADUATE
PUBLISHING GROUP

www.thelifegraduate.com

MY FOOTY JOURNAL

I Love My
FOOTY

YOUR TEAM

Colour in your club team or the team you support

AUSTRALIAN RULES FOOTBALL
- SECTIONS - _Journal_

01 Season Goals
Write down your Top 3 Season Goals

02 Training & Game Logbook
Record your training sessions and game details

03 Season Notes
Write further details of your season to keep a record for future reference

04 Autographs & Photos
Gather the autographs and photos of team members, coaches and famous players

01
SEASON GOALS

WHAT ARE GOALS AND HOW CAN THEY HELP ME?

What is a Goal?

When we talk about 'Goals', we are not referring to kicking the footy through the two big white posts! A Goal is something that you would like to achieve. It's something that will help you improve or something that will help you to remain motivated throughout the season.

Goals can be 'short-term', that is, something that you would like to achieve in the next few days, weeks or months or 'long-term', being 1 year or a few years.

How can 'Goals' help me?

Establishing your goals is super important as it gives us something to strive for. When we have a goal in mind, we start to focus on those skills at training we need to improve on or encourages us to listen more attentively to our coaches who can help us improve to achieve our goal.

Example: Season Kicking Goal: 'I will be able to kick 25m on the run by the end of the football season.'

Notice how my goal was written as 'I will be able to...'. When setting your goals, write it out like you have already achieved the goal. This is a special secret to goal setting!

Now turn to the next page and see if you can write down 3 football season goals. Make sure you read back over your goals each week so you keep working hard to achieve them.

01 FOOTY SEASON GOALS

What is a **Goal**? A Goal is something that you would like to achieve.

Need some help?

You might like to set a goal about being able to kick on both your left and right feet? Perhaps there is a distance you would like to be able to kick by the end of the season? You might like to set a goal about making 3 tackles every game you play? These are just some examples of some goals you can set.

GOAL 1 ....

GOAL 2 ....

GOAL 3 ....

02
TRAINING & GAME LOGBOOK

TRAINING

Session 1: Date: / /   Start time   :   End time   :

Session 2: Date: / /   Start time   :   End time   :

Skills Completed
Write down the skills you worked on and developed during your training sessions.

....
....
....
....

Skills to improve
Write down areas that you can improve on for your next training session

....
....
....
....

Coach & Team Focus
Write down if your coach or team has a skill or game focus you are working on

....
....

Extra Notes
Do you have additional notes or thoughts you would like to write down?

....
....
....

GAME DAY

Date: /   /   Start time   :

Location: ....

Home Game   **Away Game**

Game Details

.... **Vs** ....

Game Result

    Total Points   Total Points

Our Score   Opposition Score

Coach Feedback

....
....
....

My Performance

Write down how you felt you contributed to the game. Did the coach provide you any personal feedback? Did you have any highlights? Did you have areas of improvement?

....
....
....
....
....

TRAINING

Session 1: Date: /   /   Start time   :   End time   :

Session 2: Date: /   /   Start time   :   End time   :

Skills Completed
Write down the skills you worked on and developed during your training sessions.

....
....
....
....

Skills to improve
Write down areas that you can improve on for your next training session

....
....
....
....

Coach & Team Focus
Write down if your coach or team has a skill or game focus you are working on

....
....

Extra Notes
Do you have additional notes or thoughts you would like to write down?

....
....
....

GAME DAY

Date: / / **Start time** :

Location: ....

Home Game ◯ **Away Game** ◯

Game Details

.... **Vs** ....

Game Result

Total Points   Total Points

Our Score   Opposition Score

Coach Feedback

....
....
....

My Performance   Write down how you felt you contributed to the game. Did the coach provide you any personal feedback? Did you have any highlights? Did you have areas of improvement?

....
....
....
....

TRAINING

Session 1: Date: / /   Start time :   End time :

Session 2: Date: / /   Start time :   End time :

Skills Completed
Write down the skills you worked on and developed during your training sessions.

....
....
....
....

Skills to improve
Write down areas that you can improve on for your next training session

....
....
....
....

Coach & Team Focus
Write down if your coach or team has a skill or game focus you are working on

....
....

Extra Notes
Do you have additional notes or thoughts you would like to write down?

....
....
....

GAME DAY

Date: / /   **Start time** :

Location: ....

Home Game   **Away Game**

Game Details

.... **Vs** ....

Game Result

        Total Points   Total Points

Our Score   Opposition Score

Coach Feedback

....
....
....

My Performance

Write down how you felt you contributed to the game. Did the coach provide you any personal feedback? Did you have any highlights? Did you have areas of improvement?

....
....
....
....
....

TRAINING

Session 1: Date: / /   Start time :   End time :

Session 2: Date: / /   Start time :   End time :

Skills Completed
Write down the skills you worked on and developed during your training sessions.

....
....
....
....

Skills to improve
Write down areas that you can improve on for your next training session

....
....
....
....

Coach & Team Focus
Write down if your coach or team has a skill or game focus you are working on

....
....

Extra Notes
Do you have additional notes or thoughts you would like to write down?

....
....
....

GAME DAY

Date: /   /   **Start time**   :

Location: ....

Home Game   **Away Game**

Game Details

.... **Vs** ....

Game Result

　　　　　Total Points　　　　　　　　　Total Points

Our Score　　　　　　Opposition Score

Coach Feedback

....
....
....

My Performance
Write down how you felt you contributed to the game. Did the coach provide you any personal feedback? Did you have any highlights? Did you have areas of improvement?

....
....
....
....
....

TRAINING

Session 1: Date: / /   Start time :   End time :

Session 2: Date: / /   Start time :   End time :

Skills Completed
Write down the skills you worked on and developed during your training sessions.

....
....
....
....

Skills to improve
Write down areas that you can improve on for your next training session

....
....
....
....

Coach & Team Focus
Write down if your coach or team has a skill or game focus you are working on

....
....

Extra Notes
Do you have additional notes or thoughts you would like to write down?

....
....
....

GAME DAY

Date: /   /   **Start time**   :

Location: ....

Home Game   **Away Game**

Game Details

.... **Vs** ....

Game Result

  Total Points   Total Points

Our Score   Opposition Score

Coach Feedback

....

....

....

My Performance   Write down how you felt you contributed to the game. Did the coach provide you any personal feedback? Did you have any highlights? Did you have areas of improvement?

....

....

....

....

....

TRAINING

Session 1: Date: / /   Start time :   End time :

Session 2: Date: / /   Start time :   End time :

Skills Completed
Write down the skills you worked on and developed during your training sessions.

....
....
....
....

Skills to improve
Write down areas that you can improve on for your next training session

....
....
....
....

Coach & Team Focus
Write down if your coach or team has a skill or game focus you are working on

....
....

Extra Notes
Do you have additional notes or thoughts you would like to write down?

....
....
....

GAME DAY

Date: /   /   Start time   :

Location: ....

Home Game   **Away Game**

Game Details

.... **Vs** ....

Game Result

       Total Points   Total Points

Our Score   Opposition Score

Coach Feedback

....
....
....

My Performance

Write down how you felt you contributed to the game. Did the coach provide you any personal feedback? Did you have any highlights? Did you have areas of improvement?

....
....
....
....
....

TRAINING

Session 1: Date: / /   Start time :   End time :

Session 2: Date: / /   Start time :   End time :

Skills Completed
Write down the skills you worked on and developed during your training sessions.

....
....
....
....

Skills to improve
Write down areas that you can improve on for your next training session

....
....
....
....

Coach & Team Focus
Write down if your coach or team has a skill or game focus you are working on

....
....

Extra Notes
Do you have additional notes or thoughts you would like to write down?

....
....
....

GAME DAY

Date: /   /   Start time   :

Location: ....

Home Game   **Away Game**

Game Details

.... **Vs** ....

Game Result

　　　　Total Points　　　　　　Total Points

Our Score　　　　　Opposition Score

Coach Feedback

....
....
....

My Performance   Write down how you felt you contributed to the game. Did the coach provide you any personal feedback? Did you have any highlights? Did you have areas of improvement?

....
....
....
....
....

TRAINING

Session 1: Date: / /   Start time :   End time :

Session 2: Date: / /   Start time :   End time :

Skills Completed
Write down the skills you worked on and developed during your training sessions.

....
....
....
....

Skills to improve
Write down areas that you can improve on for your next training session

....
....
....
....

Coach & Team Focus
Write down if your coach or team has a skill or game focus you are working on

....
....

Extra Notes
Do you have additional notes or thoughts you would like to write down?

....
....
....

GAME DAY

Date: /   /   Start time   :

Location: ....

Home Game   **Away Game**

Game Details

.... **Vs** ....

Game Result

　　　　Total Points　　　　　　　　Total Points

Our Score　　　　　Opposition Score

Coach Feedback

....
....
....

My Performance   Write down how you felt you contributed to the game. Did the coach provide you any personal feedback? Did you have any highlights? Did you have areas of improvement?

....
....
....
....
....

TRAINING

Session 1: Date: / /   Start time   :   End time   :

Session 2: Date: / /   Start time   :   End time   :

Skills Completed
Write down the skills you worked on and developed during your training sessions.

....
....
....
....

Skills to improve
Write down areas that you can improve on for your next training session

....
....
....
....

Coach & Team Focus
Write down if your coach or team has a skill or game focus you are working on

....
....

Extra Notes
Do you have additional notes or thoughts you would like to write down?

....
....
....

GAME DAY

Date: /   /   **Start time**   :

Location: ....

Home Game ⬡   **Away Game** ⬡

Game Details

.... **Vs** ....

Game Result

      Total Points   Total Points

Our Score   Opposition Score

Coach Feedback

....
....
....

My Performance

Write down how you felt you contributed to the game. Did the coach provide you any personal feedback? Did you have any highlights? Did you have areas of improvement?

....
....
....
....
....

TRAINING

Session 1: Date: / /   Start time   :   End time   :

Session 2: Date: / /   Start time   :   End time   :

Skills Completed
Write down the skills you worked on and developed during your training sessions.

....
....
....
....

Skills to improve
Write down areas that you can improve on for your next training session

....
....
....
....

Coach & Team Focus
Write down if your coach or team has a skill or game focus you are working on

....
....

Extra Notes
Do you have additional notes or thoughts you would like to write down?

....
....
....

GAME DAY

Date: /   /   Start time   :

Location: ....

Home Game   **Away Game**

Game Details

.... **Vs** ....

Game Result

      Total Points   Total Points

Our Score   Opposition Score

Coach Feedback

....
....
....

My Performance

Write down how you felt you contributed to the game. Did the coach provide you any personal feedback? Did you have any highlights? Did you have areas of improvement?

....
....
....
....
....

TRAINING

Session 1: Date: / /   Start time   :   End time   :

Session 2: Date: / /   Start time   :   End time   :

Skills Completed
Write down the skills you worked on and developed during your training sessions.

....

....

....

....

Skills to improve
Write down areas that you can improve on for your next training session

....

....

....

....

Coach & Team Focus
Write down if your coach or team has a skill or game focus you are working on

....

....

Extra Notes
Do you have additional notes or thoughts you would like to write down?

....

....

....

GAME DAY

Date: /   /   **Start time**   :

Location: ....

Home Game ○   **Away Game** ○

Game Details

.... **Vs** ....

Game Result

　　　Total Points　　　　　　　　Total Points

Our Score　　　　　　Opposition Score

Coach Feedback

....
....
....

My Performance   Write down how you felt you contributed to the game. Did the coach provide you any personal feedback? Did you have any highlights? Did you have areas of improvement?

....
....
....
....
....
....

TRAINING

Session 1: Date: / /   Start time :   End time :

Session 2: Date: / /   Start time :   End time :

Skills Completed
Write down the skills you worked on and developed during your training sessions.

....
....
....
....

Skills to improve
Write down areas that you can improve on for your next training session

....
....
....
....

Coach & Team Focus
Write down if your coach or team has a skill or game focus you are working on

....
....

Extra Notes
Do you have additional notes or thoughts you would like to write down?

....
....
....

GAME DAY

Date: /   /   **Start time**   :

Location: ....

Home Game   **Away Game**

Game Details

.... **Vs** ....

Game Result

　　　　Total Points　　　　　　　　　　Total Points

Our Score　　　　　　　Opposition Score

Coach Feedback

....
....
....

My Performance   Write down how you felt you contributed to the game. Did the coach provide you any personal feedback? Did you have any highlights? Did you have areas of improvement?

....
....
....
....
....

TRAINING

Session 1: Date: / /   Start time   :   End time   :

Session 2: Date: / /   Start time   :   End time   :

Skills Completed
Write down the skills you worked on and developed during your training sessions.

....
....
....
....

Skills to improve
Write down areas that you can improve on for your next training session

....
....
....
....

Coach & Team Focus
Write down if your coach or team has a skill or game focus you are working on

....
....

Extra Notes
Do you have additional notes or thoughts you would like to write down?

....
....
....

GAME DAY

Date: /   /   **Start time**   :

Location: ....

Home Game   **Away Game**

Game Details

.... **Vs** ....

Game Result

　　　Total Points　　　　　　　　　Total Points

Our Score　　　　　　Opposition Score

Coach Feedback

....
....
....

My Performance Write down how you felt you contributed to the game. Did the coach provide you any personal feedback? Did you have any highlights? Did you have areas of improvement?

....
....
....
....
....

TRAINING

Session 1: Date: / /   Start time   :   End time   :

Session 2: Date: / /   Start time   :   End time   :

Skills Completed
Write down the skills you worked on and developed during your training sessions.

....
....
....
....

Skills to improve
Write down areas that you can improve on for your next training session

....
....
....
....

Coach & Team Focus
Write down if your coach or team has a skill or game focus you are working on

....
....

Extra Notes
Do you have additional notes or thoughts you would like to write down?

....
....
....

GAME DAY

Date: / /   **Start time** :

Location: ....

Home Game   **Away Game**

Game Details

.... **Vs** ....

Game Result

　　Total Points　　　　　　　　Total Points

Our Score　　　　　Opposition Score

Coach Feedback

....
....
....

My Performance
Write down how you felt you contributed to the game. Did the coach provide you any personal feedback? Did you have any highlights? Did you have areas of improvement?

....
....
....
....
....

TRAINING

Session 1: Date: / /   Start time :   End time :

Session 2: Date: / /   Start time :   End time :

Skills Completed
Write down the skills you worked on and developed during your training sessions.

....
....
....
....

Skills to improve
Write down areas that you can improve on for your next training session

....
....
....
....

Coach & Team Focus
Write down if your coach or team has a skill or game focus you are working on

....
....

Extra Notes
Do you have additional notes or thoughts you would like to write down?

....
....
....

GAME DAY

Date: / /   **Start time**   :

Location: ....

Home Game   **Away Game**

Game Details

.... **Vs** ....

Game Result

　　　　Total Points　　　　　　　　　　Total Points

Our Score　　　　　　Opposition Score

Coach Feedback

....
....
....

My Performance   Write down how you felt you contributed to the game. Did the coach provide you any personal feedback? Did you have any highlights? Did you have areas of improvement?

....
....
....
....
....

TRAINING

Session 1: Date: /   /   Start time   :   End time   :

Session 2: Date: /   /   Start time   :   End time   :

Skills Completed   Write down the skills you worked on and developed during your training sessions.

....

....

....

....

Skills to improve   Write down areas that you can improve on for your next training session

....

....

....

....

Coach & Team Focus   Write down if your coach or team has a skill or game focus you are working on

....

....

Extra Notes   Do you have additional notes or thoughts you would like to write down?

....

....

....

GAME DAY

Date: /   /   **Start time**   :

Location: ....

Home Game   **Away Game**

Game Details

.... **Vs** ....

Game Result

　　　　Total Points　　　　　　　　Total Points

Our Score　　　　　　Opposition Score

Coach Feedback

....
....
....

My Performance
Write down how you felt you contributed to the game. Did the coach provide you any personal feedback? Did you have any highlights? Did you have areas of improvement?

....
....
....
....

TRAINING

Session 1: Date: / /   Start time :   End time :

Session 2: Date: / /   Start time :   End time :

Skills Completed
Write down the skills you worked on and developed during your training sessions.

....
....
....
....

Skills to improve
Write down areas that you can improve on for your next training session

....
....
....
....

Coach & Team Focus
Write down if your coach or team has a skill or game focus you are working on

....
....

Extra Notes
Do you have additional notes or thoughts you would like to write down?

....
....
....

GAME DAY

Date: /   /   Start time   :

Location: ....

Home Game   **Away Game**

Game Details

.... **Vs** ....

Game Result

        Total Points   Total Points

Our Score   Opposition Score

Coach Feedback

....

....

....

My Performance

Write down how you felt you contributed to the game. Did the coach provide you any personal feedback? Did you have any highlights? Did you have areas of improvement?

....

....

....

....

....

TRAINING

Session 1: Date: / /   Start time   :   End time   :

Session 2: Date: / /   Start time   :   End time   :

Skills Completed
Write down the skills you worked on and developed during your training sessions.

....
....
....
....

Skills to improve
Write down areas that you can improve on for your next training session

....
....
....
....

Coach & Team Focus
Write down if your coach or team has a skill or game focus you are working on

....
....

Extra Notes
Do you have additional notes or thoughts you would like to write down?

....
....
....

GAME DAY

Date: / /   Start time   :

Location: ....

Home Game   **Away Game**

Game Details

.... **Vs** ....

Game Result

　　　　Total Points　　　　　　　　Total Points

Our Score　　　　　Opposition Score

Coach Feedback

....
....
....

My Performance
Write down how you felt you contributed to the game. Did the coach provide you any personal feedback? Did you have any highlights? Did you have areas of improvement?

....
....
....
....
....

TRAINING

Session 1: Date: / /   Start time :   End time :

Session 2: Date: / /   Start time :   End time :

Skills Completed
Write down the skills you worked on and developed during your training sessions.

....
....
....
....

Skills to improve
Write down areas that you can improve on for your next training session

....
....
....
....

Coach & Team Focus
Write down if your coach or team has a skill or game focus you are working on

....
....

Extra Notes
Do you have additional notes or thoughts you would like to write down?

....
....
....

GAME DAY

Date: /   /   Start time   :

Location: ....

Home Game   **Away Game**

Game Details

.... **Vs** ....

Game Result

　　　Total Points　　　　　　Total Points

Our Score　　　　　Opposition Score

Coach Feedback

....
....
....

My Performance

Write down how you felt you contributed to the game. Did the coach provide you any personal feedback? Did you have any highlights? Did you have areas of improvement?

....
....
....
....
....

TRAINING

Session 1: Date: / /   Start time   :   End time   :

Session 2: Date: / /   Start time   :   End time   :

Skills Completed
Write down the skills you worked on and developed during your training sessions.

....
....
....
....

Skills to improve
Write down areas that you can improve on for your next training session

....
....
....
....

Coach & Team Focus
Write down if your coach or team has a skill or game focus you are working on

....
....

Extra Notes
Do you have additional notes or thoughts you would like to write down?

....
....
....

GAME DAY

Date: / /   **Start time** :

Location: ....

Home Game   **Away Game**

Game Details

.... **Vs** ....

Game Result

Total Points   Total Points

Our Score   Opposition Score

Coach Feedback

....
....
....

My Performance
Write down how you felt you contributed to the game. Did the coach provide you any personal feedback? Did you have any highlights? Did you have areas of improvement?

....
....
....
....
....

TRAINING

Session 1: Date: / /   Start time   :   End time   :

Session 2: Date: / /   Start time   :   End time   :

Skills Completed
Write down the skills you worked on and developed during your training sessions.

....

....

....

....

Skills to improve
Write down areas that you can improve on for your next training session

....

....

....

....

Coach & Team Focus
Write down if your coach or team has a skill or game focus you are working on

....

....

Extra Notes
Do you have additional notes or thoughts you would like to write down?

....

....

....

GAME DAY

Date: /   /   Start time   :

Location: ....

Home Game   **Away Game**

Game Details

.... **Vs** ....

Game Result

       Total Points   Total Points

Our Score   Opposition Score

Coach Feedback

....
....
....

My Performance

Write down how you felt you contributed to the game. Did the coach provide you any personal feedback? Did you have any highlights? Did you have areas of improvement?

....
....
....
....
....

TRAINING

Session 1: Date: / /   Start time :   End time :

Session 2: Date: / /   Start time :   End time :

Skills Completed
Write down the skills you worked on and developed during your training sessions.

....
....
....
....

Skills to improve
Write down areas that you can improve on for your next training session

....
....
....
....

Coach & Team Focus
Write down if your coach or team has a skill or game focus you are working on

....
....

Extra Notes
Do you have additional notes or thoughts you would like to write down?

....
....
....

GAME DAY

Date: /   /   Start time   :

Location: ....

Home Game   **Away Game**

Game Details

.... **Vs** ....

Game Result

       Total Points   Total Points

Our Score   Opposition Score

Coach Feedback

....
....
....

My Performance
Write down how you felt you contributed to the game. Did the coach provide you any personal feedback? Did you have any highlights? Did you have areas of improvement?

....
....
....
....
....

TRAINING

Session 1: Date: / /   Start time :   End time :

Session 2: Date: / /   Start time :   End time :

Skills Completed
Write down the skills you worked on and developed during your training sessions.

....
....
....
....

Skills to improve
Write down areas that you can improve on for your next training session

....
....
....
....

Coach & Team Focus
Write down if your coach or team has a skill or game focus you are working on

....
....

Extra Notes
Do you have additional notes or thoughts you would like to write down?

....
....
....

GAME DAY

Date: /   /   Start time   :

Location: ....

Home Game   **Away Game**

Game Details

.... **Vs** ....

Game Result

　　　　Total Points　　　　　　　　Total Points

Our Score　　　　　　Opposition Score

Coach Feedback

....
....
....

My Performance   Write down how you felt you contributed to the game. Did the coach provide you any personal feedback? Did you have any highlights? Did you have areas of improvement?

....
....
....
....
....

03

SEASON NOTES

NOTES

Do you have any season notes that you would like to add? Were there any highlights? Is there an area of your game you would like to improve on for next season?

....

....

....

....

....

....

....

....

....

....

....

....

....

....

....

NOTES

Do you have any season notes that you would like to add? Were there any highlights? Is there an area of your game you would like to improve on for next season?

....

....

....

....

....

....

....

....

....

....

....

....

....

....

....

NOTES

Do you have any season notes that you would like to add? Were there any highlights? Is there an area of your game you would like to improve on for next season?

....

....

....

....

....

....

....

....

....

....

....

....

....

....

....

04

Autographs & Photos

Autographs & Photo's

Autographs & Photo's

Autographs & Photo's

Autographs & Photo's

Autographs & Photo's

Autographs & Photo's

My Australian Rules Football Journal

The Life Graduate
PUBLISHING GROUP

www.ingramcontent.com/pod-product-compliance
Lightning Source LLC
LaVergne TN
LVHW060215080526
838202LV00052B/4283